Hansel and his sister, lived with their and in a little  on the edge of the .

One day their told their , "There is no longer enough food for all of us to eat. Tomorrow we must take  and  into the  and leave them there. If we don't we shall all starve."

Their  was very sad but at last he agreed.

 overheard them talking so he crept outside and filled his pockets with white pebbles.

The next day their  and  took the children deep into the . They lit a fire and told  and  to rest while they went to chop wood.

 and  curled up and

fell asleep. When they awoke
they were alone in the dark.

"Do not be afraid ," said , "for I have left a trail of white pebbles. When the rises, we shall easily find our way back home."

Their was very happy to see his children. Not so their . When she noticed the trail, she locked them in their room so that they could not gather any more pebbles.

The next morning the children were each given a crust of bread to eat.

Once again they were taken deep into the forest. had broken his into crumbs to leave a trail, but when the rose, the children found that the of the had eaten all the breadcrumbs.

They were lost!

 and  wandered even deeper into the  looking for their way home.

At last, when and could go no further, they saw a little through the . To their delight the children found that the was made of gingerbread. and each helped themselves to a piece of the roof.

It tasted delicious! Just at that moment a kind appeared at the front door.

The  took and

inside where a delicious meal

of and was waiting.

Then she tucked them into

two little .

But the kind was really

a wicked in disguise!

The next morning the

woke the children roughly. She

locked in a cage. Then

she told , "You must work

very hard cooking for .
When he has fattened up, I
shall roast and eat him!"

Every morning the 🧙 went to the cage and said to 🧒, "Stretch out your finger so that I may tell whether you are fat enough to roast yet."

Now, witches have very small red 👁 👁 and cannot see very far. So 🧒 stuck out an old 🦴 instead! The 🧙 was very puzzled because he never seemed to get any fatter.

The day came when the could wait no longer.

She lit her big old .
Then she said to , "Climb
inside my dear to see if it is
hot enough to bake ."

realized that very soon
the wicked meant to roast
her, too, so she replied, "But
I do not know how and the
is far too small."

The 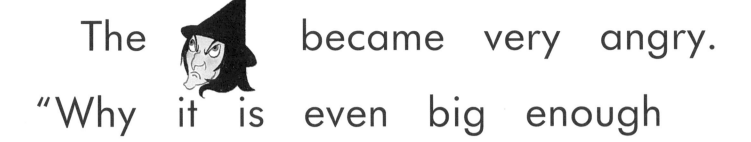 became very angry.
"Why it is even big enough

for me," she snapped. Then she put her head right into the  to show .

Just at that moment,  pushed the  with all her might! The  fell right into the  and then quickly locked the !

 ran to free  from the cage and tell him that the wicked  was dead.

Now that there was nothing more to fear and went to explore the old witch's secret room. In every nook and cranny they found sparkling piles of and . The children filled their pockets and then they set out through the hoping to find their way back home.

At long last and saw their own little through the .

Their was very pleased to see and again. He had been so unhappy since his children had been gone, and their was now dead. and gave their all the and that they had found in the gingerbread . From that day on they lived happily together in the little .